TEACH ME
TO PRAY

TEACH ME TO PRAY

W. E. Sangster

UPPER
ROOM BOOKS
NASHVILLE

Interior Design: Charles Sutherland
Twenty-third printing: 2000

The Upper Room® Web Site: http://www.upperroom.org
UPPER ROOM®, UPPER ROOM BOOKS®, and design logos are trademarks owned by The Upper Room®, Nashville, Tennessee. All rights reserved.

Library of Congress Catalog Card Number: 59-15667

Previously published in Great Britain by the Epworth Press under the titles: *Teach Us to Pray, How to Form a Prayer Cell,* and *How to Live in Christ.* Used by permission.

Foreword

≫

I never knew Dr. Sangster, except through his extraordinary writing. I first read *Teach Me to Pray* in 1980 after a weekend prayer experience in my church that was sponsored by The Upper Room. I was deeply impressed by the authenticity and the practicality of the author's spiritual counsel. This book, I remember thinking to myself, could only have been written by one who lived the life of which he wrote.

As it turned out, my intuition was right. Until he died in 1960, Dr. Sangster was widely regarded as one of the world's greatest religious leaders and spiritual writers.

The Upper Room first published *Teach Me to Pray* in 1959, though the material had by then already enjoyed a wide reading in religious circles in England and in the USA in the form of three independent essays. Over the past forty years, *Teach Me to Pray* has sic among many, including myself, because of the enduring and genuine quality of Dr. Sangster's counsel. By now, millions of spiritual pilgrims have benefitted from reading *Teach Me to Pray* in the English, Spanish and Korean languages.

Over the years, I have returned again and again to this little handbook on the spiritual life. I have given copies to countless others as they have expressed to me their hunger for communion with God, for help in learning to pray, and for guidance in living their lives in Christ. *Teach Me to Pray* has indeed become one of my special companions in prayer.

Part I, *Teach Me to Pray*, deals with the practice of prayer. Dr. Sangster is concerned with helping beginners, which includes most all of us. Even those who have been praying for a long time will find great benefit in the discussion of two common obstacles to a life of prayer as well as the practice of a rule of prayer. Dr. Sangster draws on the best of our ancient and contemporary spiritual heritage as he offers practical counsel for the practices of listening prayer, intercession, and meditation.

Part II, How to Form a Prayer Cell, deals with the formation of prayer groups and the fostering a prayer movement across our land. Dr. Sangster believed that God renews the church where people are gathering together to seek God's will in prayer—in the church, in the home, at work, and in every other setting where people live and relate. Millions of people neglect prayer because they think it is 'just pious talk' when we ought to be active and busy with serving others. Dr. Sangster declares, "Only when people listen to God can they learn what they should be 'up and doing.' "

Part III, How to Live in Christ, deals with the essence of the Christian life—life lived in Christ. The phrase comes from Paul. Paul writes of being in Christ and of having Christ in us. For Dr. Sangster, life in Christ is not an abstraction, but a lived reality that requires practice and practical guidance. Only as Christ lives in more and more people will the world be changed. Dr. Sangster reminds us that giving our minds to Christ is not as difficult as it may appear. "All our school days our teachers urge us 'to give our minds' to things—We give our minds to Christ when we attend to him, think of him, walk with him—and the more we give our minds, the more he gives us his."

The content of this little book is transformational for those who take to heart and practice what is here. May God be with you in your journey of prayer and life with Christ.

—Stephen D. Bryant

Contents

Part III: How to Live in Christ
65

THIS BOOK
will do you no good unless you read it.

THIS BOOK
will do you limited good if you only read it.

THIS BOOK
could do you great good if you studied it.

THIS BOOK
could change your life if it taught you to pray.

PART 1

Teach Me to Pray

He was praying in a certain place, and after he had finished, one of his disciples said to him, "Lord, teach us to pray."

—Luke 11:1

Part I: Teach Me to Pray

❧

Our Neglect of Prayer

I have often heard it said by thoughtful people that all the Church's problems can be traced to our neglect of prayer. The statement is probably a little exaggerated, but contains enough truth to warrant careful scrutiny. Is it a fact that we are praying less than we did?

Certainly prayer meetings are less common than they were in the spacious days of evangelical religion. Plenty of reasons could be given for the decay of the prayer meeting—and not all of them bad ones—but I am dealing now, not with causes, but with facts. The prayer meeting is by no means as common as it was once.

Family prayer, as far as my observation goes, is less common, too. Here and there the sweet custom survives, but it has ceased to be the practice even in Christian homes. It may be the conviction that prayer is a very *private* thing that has led to the decay of the custom, or the fear in the mind of a sensitive host that a guest in the home might be embarrassed if invited to join in prayer. I do not know. But keeping again to the facts rather than the causes, it seems clear that family prayer is no longer a general practice, even among devout people.

What of private prayer? Is that decaying too?

Who can say? Being private, no one can know.

Yet I believe (writing with a sense of responsibility and after much thought) that the same is true here also. The lack of eagerness for prayer meetings and family prayer might seem to point that way, but it could not prove it. I am more impressed by the fact that after nearly thirty years of ministry, much of which has been given to personal interviews with people about the health of their soul, hundreds and hundreds have admitted to me that they had no disciplined prayer life worthy of the name. Some even rationalized their neglect and argued that it did not matter so long as they were good. Many were still in the kindergarten of the school of prayer, and some consistently rushed through all their intercourse with heaven.

There will, of course, be thousands of souls who are much drawn out in prayer and may even pattern themselves in this regard on the greatest figures of the past. I know at least one devout and very busy man who gives three hours a day to intercession. But, surveying the Church as a whole, and admitting the difficulty of reaching certainty in any judgment on this subject, I say in pain but in certainty that our prayer life appears to be unworthy of our Christian profession. This lack of prayer life might almost indicate doubt in our mind of the real accessibility of God in Jesus Christ.

Now, this is *very* serious. There is no progress in religion without prayer. We can be sure of this both by the testimony of the saints and the experience of the Church. All those who have gone forward with God have gone forward by prayer. There are some things on which the saints do not agree. But they agree on this: Prayer—and more prayer! If you would be close to God, there is no other way than prayer.

The experience of the Church confirms this. Periods of spiritual power in the Church have been preceded by, and sustained by, great prayer. There are many unsolved problems of prayer, but the greater need of those of us who profess to believe in it is more of the *practice* of prayer. No limit can be put to its power. While some of the problems still remain unsolved, prayer *does* things. We do not fully know *how*, but often God uses it to heal the body. Prayer cannot add points to your IQ, but it clears and sharp-

17

ens the minds of millions of men and women. It is the only way to the sanctifying of the soul.

I grow more and more sure of the supreme importance of prayer. I know as a minister that I have failed my people most, not in my preaching or pastoral work, but in my prayer. Yet anyone may enter this "Order": male or female; clergy or lay; sick or well.

Let us think together about prayer—not the problems of it, but the practice of it. How would we answer people who approached us in the way the disciple approached the Lord and said: "Teach us to pray"?

SINCERITY IS NOT ENOUGH

I am afraid I may have startled and even shocked some who are reading this by the statement I made that a busy friend of mine spends three hours a day in prayer.

Let no one be intimidated by that. He is on the most intimate terms with God and would suffer the sharpest distress if any disclosure of his practice so overwhelmed a novice that the novice lost all heart to begin at all. Fifteen minutes in the morning and ten at night, consistently adhered to, would begin to make amazing differences in the life of any man or woman.

Yet even that amount of time seems too long to some people. Years ago, a student confessed to me his inability to pray beyond five minutes. It was his habit, it seemed, to pray only at night. He asked to be forgiven for anything he had done wrong, gave thanks for God's blessings, mentioned his mother and father and certain of his friends, and in five minutes there was not another relevant thought in his mind. How people could pray for hours was a mystery beyond his understanding.

Our thinking on prayer will always be small if we limit it largely to petition.

I was in a women's meeting the other day. It was lovely to hear those good women warm the church and warm their own hearts by singing their choruses. They sang with special fervor one entitled "A Little Talk with Jesus Makes It Right, All Right."

Would that do as a definition of prayer?

It would, in a way, and God forbid that I should seem so technical about prayer that I left folk supposing it was like a doctor's prescription, and would be wrong if even one element were omitted. But truth compels me to affirm that "a little talk with Jesus" could be very self-centered, very narrow, and, among other omissions, leave no room at all for listening.

Some folk speak as though the only thing required to make prayer holy is to be sure that it is sincere.

But the test is not stern enough. We can be sincere *and selfish*. Think of the classic prayer found among the papers of John Ward, Member of Parliament, who, many, many years ago, owned a variety of properties in England:

"O Lord, Thou knowest I have mine estates in the City of London, and likewise that I have lately purchased an estate in fee-simple in the County of Essex. I beseech Thee to preserve the two counties of Middlesex and Essex from fire and earthquake, and, as I have a mortgage in Hertfordshire, I beg of Thee likewise to have an eye of compassion on that county; for the rest of the counties, Thou mayest deal with them as Thou art pleased. . . ."

It is impossible to doubt the sincerity of this prayer, yet it is anything but holy. Prayer, properly understood, is not just petition, or a little talk with Jesus, or the outpouring of sincere selfishness: it has range and richness and sweep. A child can use it, but the profoundest saint cannot get to the bottom of it. It is, indeed, the highest activity of which mortals are capable. It is learning to know God at firsthand. It is the sovereign way to holiness. It is the royal road to assurance.

So much religion, alas! is secondhand. So many people live a parasitic life on the faith of others. They believe in God because someone else they admire holds the faith with firmness; so their belief is a very vague one. Such a religion will not comfort them when "waves and storms go o'er their head."

What would it be worth to you in this atomic age to be utterly *sure* of God?

What would it be worth to you when you are beaten by sin and "weary of passions unsubdued" to feel the conquering power of God mounting within your soul?

Prayer is the way. All progress in religion centers in prayer.

FEELING IS NO GUIDE TO PRAYING

Many people want to pray well, but find themselves strangely hindered. The two chief hindrances are enslavement to feeling and wandering thoughts. If we could find the way over those obstacles, the journey would be well begun.

Some people take it for granted that it is no good to pray unless you "feel like it." They believe that the worth of prayer depends upon our emotional fervor at the time.

So far is that from being true that the precise opposite comes nearer the truth. Our prayers offered when we *do not* feel like it are more acceptable than those offered when we do. Nor is it hard to understand why.

When we pray because we feel like it, we are pleasing ourselves. We want to pray and we *do* pray, and our prayer is acceptable to God in the degree that our will is in harmony with God's will.

But by praying when we do not feel like it, we bring God not only the content of our prayer, but a disciplined spirit. We have kept our appointment with God *against* inclination. We have displeased ourselves in order to please God, and God's pleasure is real indeed.

Feelings can be very sweet, and never to know the rapture of religion would be dreadful. But feelings are too insubstantial and too variable to be the guide to our praying. Feeling fluctuates with our health, our temperaments, the weather, the news. It fluctuates also with what we eat and with whom we met last! Our commerce with heaven cannot depend on things so fortuitous as that.

Forbes Robinson—a master of prayer—said:

"Do not mind about feelings. You may have beautiful feelings. Thank God if you have. He sends them. You may have none. Thank God if you have not, for He has kept them back. We do not want to *feel* better and stronger: we want to *be* better and stronger. . . ."

If in time past you have prayed only when you felt like it, pause now and take a vow. Vow to keep your appointment with God whether you feel like it or not. You would not fail to keep an appointment with another person because the inclination had ebbed when the hour of meeting had come. Courtesy would carry you there if desire did not.

Can you be less courteous with God?

But how shall we deal with ourselves if, when the time for prayer has come, our feelings are at low tide? Can desire be enlivened? Is there some simple technique to inflame the longing for prayer?

George Müller found that a few well-chosen verses from the Bible quietly brooded on would at any time warm the spirit of prayer in him. Many Christians in the last two hundred years have come to their communion with God through a hymn. A hymn a day keeps the devil away! Others have spent a few minutes with a book of devotion—though people vary a great deal, I find, in the devotional book which helps them most. With some it is an old book like Thomas à Kempis' *Imitation of Christ*, or William Law's *Serious Call*, or Brother Lawrence's *Practice of the Presence of God*. With others, it is a modern book like Oswald Chambers' *My Utmost for His Highest*, or Stanley Jones's *The Way of Abundant Living*.

Some folk are quite independent of books in this matter. They kindle the desire to pray by a simple meditation. They make their minds quiet and picture the cross. They see their Lord dying because of sin. A sense of unpayable debt grows in their hearts and halting words of love fall from their lips. Or they concentrate in thought on the privilege of being able to pray at all, and they see themselves talking to God as though God were with them in the room. The amazing truth breaks over them in waves of wonder, and prayer leaps out because it must.

But suppose, *even then*, that the spirit is so cold and dead that none of these strategies succeed? What then?

Keep the appointment just the same. Do not pretend! Tell God, if you like, that you have no inclination to prayer, and that you have dragged yourself to your knees.

Still you will be welcome. God remembers that we are dust.

WANDERING THOUGHTS

I said just now that the second greatest hindrance to prayer is wandering thoughts. I cannot honestly promise that even the most devout will ever have a complete deliverance from this. One's power to remain concentrated in prayer will grow, and skill in outwitting the bias of the mind to roam away will increase also; but if I am to go by the testimony of the ripest saints, a permanent emancipation from this difficulty is not to be expected on earth.

But most of us can have a greater mastery over wandering thoughts than we enjoy at present. Concentration and consecration are nearer together than we know.

One of the chief dangers of this breathless age is that we shall come to our prayers breathless also. Babbling one's prayers is a poor occupation at any time—even if the babbling is not vocalized and we just rush through them in our mind. Let us learn to be quiet within: to come to God, however brief our time of prayer, unhurried; to be *still* before God, recognizing that the day has nothing more important than this intercourse with heaven.

I may help someone if I confess that my own battle with wandering thoughts turns chiefly on the many engagements that each day brings. The quiet of prayer is invaded by the thought of a mass of correspondence to be handled; a cluttered desk awaiting my attention; *this* duty, *that* duty. These distractions seem to stand row on row, bidding me leave the quiet and get on with my work—always with the subtle insinuation that the work is more important than the prayer!

I have learned through the years how to outwit that kind of distraction. Instead of fighting those thoughts away, I lift them right into my prayers. I go through the whole day slowly with God, meeting my duties in prayer before I meet them in fact. I have two immense gains from that discipline. When I have looked them in the face in that way, they lie down and do not interrupt the rest of my prayers. Then when I come to deal with the duties that I have already met in reverent imagination, I seem more the master of them and better able to make those duties of maximum usefulness for God.

This, also, I have found of use. I made a distinction just now between mental and vocal prayer. Most of our private prayers are mental: we offer them to God *in our mind*.

But when one is able to pray alone, it helps in the battle against wandering thoughts to offer the prayer on a breath: to murmur it, however quietly, *aloud*. Somehow, the lips and the ears come to the aid of the mind and with power beat back the distracting thoughts.

Nevertheless, it must be admitted that there are days when all this ingenuity seems unavailing, when the mind is in a vagrant mood and darts off from the firm line of prayer by the oddest associations. What are we to do then?

Firmly pull the mind back again! The moment you realize you are off the straight, sanctify the wandering thought, if you can, with a prayer for the thing to which it has wandered, but resolutely bring your mind back to the theme of your directed praying. On some days the whole period of prayer will pass in this effort at concentration and you will be tempted to believe that the time has been wasted. In point of fact, the time has been well spent. You have splendidly exercised the muscles of the will, and have made more frequent the periods when concentration will be easy, and, without much effort in the mind itself, your soul is caught up in God.

Much of my time is spent on trains. Often they are crowded. Chatter goes on for hours. Yet this train car must be my study and sometimes my prayer room. When the normal civilities are over, I put my mind on my work or my meditation; and *I do not hear the rest*. It is possible to be in a state of concentration, mental and spiritual. The knowledge that God can do that for us should beckon us all along our pilgrim way.

A RULE OF PRAYER

People have often asked me for a "plan" of prayer—some simple sequence in which they might feel that every legitimate element in prayer was given its place, and in the richness of which they would find ten minutes too short rather than five minutes too long.

I think it is a fair request, and I will attempt to meet it if we agree that our first thoughts on waking and our last thoughts before sleeping shall be given to God, and that we give God also fifteen minutes as early in the day as possible and ten minutes more at its close.

On waking: Turn your thoughts at once to God. Murmur to yourself: "Praise God from whom all blessings flow," or "This is the day the Lord has made: I will rejoice and be glad in it," or "Christ, whose glory fills the skies. . . ."

1. Morning Prayer

Plan for fifteen minutes as a minimum in the morning, and as early as possible. Here is a rule of prayer I have found helpful myself:

Adoration: Think of the greatness of God—how incredible it is that God should hear us at all. Does not the wonder of it almost strike you speechless? Praise be to God that God is the God God is!

Thanksgiving: Go over your mercies. They are more than you know. Thank God for health, home, love, work, friends, books, fun, a night's rest. . . . If you lack health, or home, or sleep, there are other great mercies to mention. Think on them until you glow with gratitude.

Dedication: You are already dedicated to God with whole-life vows. Nonetheless, follow the lead of the hymn writer: "That vow renewed shall daily hear." You are not your own. Nothing you have is your own. You are a "given" man or woman.

Guidance: Ask God for guidance all through the day. Forethink and foresee your day with God. In imagination go over every task that you know the day has in store for you and meet it with God. Even the things you cannot foresee will be better met because of this discipline.

Intercession: Pray for others. Have a prayer list. Praying without method is not serious prayer. When you get to heaven and realize all that prayer did on this earth, you will be ashamed that you prayed so poorly. The casual recollection of people in need, or prayers only for one's dear ones, or prayers too general—common weaknesses as these are—can all be overcome by a prayer list kept up to date and used daily.

Petition: Some masters of prayer have no place for personal petition. Clement of Alexandria had none. He and many like him were content to let God give them what was good. Yet Jesus taught petition—and that is enough. But keep petition in a minor place. Nothing more reveals the childishness of our prayers than praying with persistence and passion only when we want something for ourselves!

Meditation: It is a good thing to conclude prayer, as well as to begin it, with meditation: deep brooding on love, wisdom, beauty, joy, light, peace, power, freedom, and holiness. A hymn may help you here.

2. Evening Prayer

Plan for ten minutes as a minimum at the end of the day.

Review the day: Run over it backwards in the recollected presence of God, and you will almost certainly have a double need.

Confession: Things will come to your mind that will not be pleasant to recall. A failure here; a bit of posing there; something not *strictly* truthful; exaggeration; and missed opportunities for doing good. . . . Deal with each separately. Itemize your sins. Do not bundle your beastliness or pettiness together in one of those all-inclusive phrases, "Forgive me all my sins"; but blush over them in their separateness, claiming forgiveness and a great wariness in the future. Make restitution where you can.

Thanksgiving: Every evening will bring its occasion for gratitude to God for morning prayers answered and for help through the day. Let the day close with a warm, inward awareness that God has, indeed, been with you "all through the day."

Before sleeping: Commit yourself to God again. "Father, into your hands I commend my spirit."

> Be my last thought, how sweet to rest
> For ever on my Savior's breast.

Last thoughts often color our dreams; and we, like the Christians of the eighteenth century, have need to pray: "O God, make my dreams holy."

GETTING GUIDANCE

People who have any maturity in the spiritual life know that there is a *listening* side to prayer. Not all prayer is made up of our human speaking. "God is not dumb that he should speak no more." It is both courteous and highly profitable not only to talk but to listen to God.

God guides us in many ways. God guides through the Bible and the teaching of the Church, through the counsel of Christian parents and friends. But what I am most concerned to discuss on prayer is the direct counsel that can come from the mind of God to the mind of a devout soul who listens to the Almighty. Those people who say it is "all nonsense" because they have had no experience of it are denying a mass of testimony from the saints and denying the plain teaching of the Bible, also. Said Isaiah: "Your ears shall hear a word behind you, saying, 'This is the way; walk in it.' "

When people are first learning to listen to God, it is worth reminding them that they do not need guidance in this way on many things. Over wide areas of life, God's will is already clear. There are Ten Commandments. There are our Lord's laws of love. The ethical standards of the New Testament are plain to anyone who will read the Book. A person might turn to God for guidance and be condemned in the light of these Commandments and by the holy Book, for God will not set the Commandments aside in answer to a bit of special pleading.

Nor should we expect, as some people appear to do, that the guidance of God will always be to the unusual. For the mass of men and women who are in the Christian way of life, and on the majority of their days, the guidance of God will run along the path of plain and known duty. They will not be constantly doing extraordinary things, but ordinary things in an extraordinary way.

Nor should we say that we are going to God for guidance when we have already made up our own minds and are seeking divine approval for what we intend to do. This great word has been demeaned by shallow use. Employ it with reserve. To say that one is guided by God is a rare and *awe-filled* thing. Let us say it, therefore, only when we are inwardly sure.

How does one prepare oneself to receive guidance from God?

You are in the spirit of prayer, withdrawn from the world. You are in the conscious presence of God. Self is no longer at the center. As things cross your mind, they have no immediate self-reference, as—alas!— they do in normal life. People normally ask, "How will that affect me?" "What do I get out of it?" But you see things differently because you see them in the light of God. Conscience is at its tenderest. Spiritual perception is sharp and penetrating. It is God and you.

Listen! Something comes—clearly, maybe, or not so clear. If it is something to do, make a note of it and get it done as soon as possible: a letter to write, a call to make, an apology possibly. With the majority of things that come there is no moral uncertainty, and critics might say, "I could have thought of those things myself." They could—but they did not. When a thing is plainly right, it is, perhaps, an academic question whether I thought of it myself or whether God told me. But one thing is certain. I thought of far, far fewer sweet things to do, and hard things, before I learned to listen to God than I do now that it is my daily practice. So perhaps it was God, after all, helping me to think!

If you feel uncertain whether what comes to you in the quietness is of God, test it by its harmony with all that you know of Jesus, and discuss it in confidence with some wise and sharp Christian friend. If the projected course, while morally sound, appears to conflict with your reasoned judgment, turn again to your sharp and believing friends. God's guidance *does* run counter at times to our best judgment. Paul's fine judgment once directed him to Bithynia; but the Spirit stopped him; and God called him *against* his judgment to Macedonia, to Europe—and to us.

What can one do when faced with two or three possible courses of action and with no certainty as to which to take?

The old Quakers, who knew a great deal about

walking by the inner light, decided usually by the test of "peace."

Go into the quiet again with God. Wait before God in utter stillness. Hold out the dilemma before the Father. Just wait!

Now—in imagination—*see* yourself traveling each of those possible roads in turn. This one . . . then that one. If there are more than two roads, these others also. Each in turn. Unhurriedly!

There may be pain in all of them, but on *one* it is probable that the "peace" will rest. As you see yourself traveling that road, whatever the cost, you will find peace in your heart.

That is your path. A voice behind you says: "This is the way; walk in it."

But do not try to *hurry* God. God may keep you waiting for assurance until the time comes to act.

INTERCESSION

I am not in any doubt that people who are advanced in the school of prayer spend more time in intercession than in any other of the segments of prayer— and often more time in intercession than in all the others put together. The need is so great. The effects can be so powerful. The sheer unselfishness of it is so compelling that it is no wonder that the weight of their intercourse with heaven falls here.

Is there anything that we can learn about intercession that will deepen our desire for it and increase our skill?

Most people need to be more *particular* and more *methodical*. By *particular*, in this connection, I mean that we ought to pray for persons more than for areas. I do not know how it is with others; but when, say, overseas missions are in my mind, I cannot pray with any sense of effectiveness for China or India. My thought splays out over those vast sub-continents, and I have a jumble of images in my mind made up of coolies and temples and elephants and teapickers. While I would not say that God can do nothing with my prayers, I know within myself that this is not praying at its best. But if I fix my mind on missionaries I know in either of those countries; inform myself of their exact situation; enter, perhaps by personal correspondence, or through a magazine or circular letter, into their personal circumstances—I can lay hold on them in their need and on God's divine power, and I can pray the blessing down.

By *methodical* I mean that we ought to keep prayer lists. I do not know how any person serious in intercession can avoid it. I am blessed with a good memory myself, but to leave the objects of our intercession to the half-casual recollections of prayer time itself will almost certainly issue in a lack of that particularity I was pleading for above, and the omission of many who justly claim a place in our prayers.

Making a prayer list is a means of grace in itself. Some people make a list to cover a month; others work on the week as a unit. Nearly all those serious intercessors have a constantly changing priority list of people in the most urgent need and for whom during their period of acute necessity they pray *every* day. Even so holy an occupation as prayer, as we have already noted, *can* tend toward self-centeredness. Confession, thanksgiving, dedication, and the plea for guidance keep the self very much in mind. Intercession carries us right away from self. As one glorious by-product of this secret intercession with God for others, we have this lovely *un*self-centeredness, and prove once more that we never do anything for others that does not bless ourselves.

Is it possible to describe, with any usefulness, our mental processes in the act of intercession itself?

Certainly we cannot use a prayer list as though it were a telephone directory, and just run our eye down a list of names. Nor is it much better, I think, to speak the names aloud, if it is all done at speed. There is more in it than that. Wait before God in the quietness. Remember God's presence, power, and love. Wait. . . .

Take a name from your list. *See* the person in your mind's eye. See him or her vividly. Gaze at him with a steady directness you might hesitate to use if you were actually face to face. Let your mind play over her circumstances and concentrate on her particular need. If it is sickness, do not wallow in the pain and other distressing details. Recognize the symptoms, but do not aim to reproduce them in your own feelings. Constantly doing that out of misguided sympathy and with a long list of sick people will make you ill yourself.

Now—with this face and need vividly in mind— think of God. Think strongly. Think of God's power and will to meet your friend's need. See your friends now (and soak in the thought!) as *God* could make them: holy, healthy, able to meet their situation and master the circumstance in which they find themselves.

Now fuse the two images: your friend in need and God, powerful and loving. Hold them together in the crucible of your desiring heart, and you can almost feel the blessing going over.

It takes time, of course. It is slow work done well, and costly in concentration. That is why prayer lists cannot be too long. That is why one ought never to ask lightly for someone else's prayers. People sometimes ask for one's prayers quite casually and with no particular need in mind. Nor do they live in expectation of any special blessing afterward. Perhaps it was just a bit of pious patter.

Yet the great intercessors remain the men and women of secret influence in all communities. To be mentioned in their prayers is incomparably more enriching than to be mentioned in their wills.

MEDITATION

I have come to the end of my message on private prayer, but I want to conclude this section with a word on meditation, which, strictly speaking, is not prayer at all.

Indeed, it is hard, in a way, to say what meditation is. One can approach it best by saying what it is *not*. It is not prayer—though it merges into it. It is not imagination—though it makes fine use of that noble gift. It is not thinking—if by thinking one means boring into a problem. It is not daydreaming— though the inexperienced often think it is. It is not autosuggestion—though some pseudo-psychologists confuse the two. It is a mental dwelling upon God that opens our nature to the divine inflow, and main-

39

tains in devout Christians what Henry Scougal called "The Life of God in the Soul of Man."

All of us have Christian friends outstanding for their poise and inward serenity. They seem to live with limitless reserves and are "all quiet within." We are disposed at times to think their happiness is explained by their good health, easy circumstances, and freedom from great trouble. But when we know them intimately, we find that some of them have immense burdens to carry, but have learned to toss their burdens on their God. Not all of them would explain their success by calling it "meditation"; but when one examines their mental habits, there is no serious doubt what it is. Their inner life is turned in trustful submission to God. They might not recognize the phrasing and "technique" of the masters of meditation. But in their own simple way they have become "contemplatives," and they have found the secret of the saints.

One of the abiding results of modern psychology is the stratification of the human mind. Discerning souls had long known, of course, of "another principle within" and "the seed of sin's disease." But despite the awkward jargon of modern psychology, there has been a real gain to thought in seeing the "strata" of one's mind: conscious, subconscious, unconscious. Plain people are coming to see that even if at times we cannot remember things, nothing is forgotten—that racial experience is in us somewhere and past personal experience is there as well. *Whatever has been, is*. Past thought and feeling sink into the subconscious, not to lie forever dormant, but to color future thought and feeling, and sometimes to rush up with terrible power to affect the will.

Some people live in the slavery of their past. All of us do to some extent. The conscious life of multitudes is colored by their immediate circumstances: the weather, the day in the week, the month of the year, the routine of the day. Wise meditation could deliver us now from this imprisonment and make our freedom more sweet with every passing month.

How do you feel when you wake on a gray winter Monday morning? The wind is driving against the bedroom window. It is quite dark or barely light. The trivial round faces you. The day may have awkward experiences in store. Depression comes over the mind like a fog. What a day! What a life!

Many people begin their day like that. The stored depressions of past days well up from memory and the working week starts with "the hump."

If one lived on *facts* and not on feelings, even the feelings would respond in time to the facts. These are the facts!

God is on the throne. Behind those rain-heavy

clouds the sun is shining, and behind the God-denying look of this mad world God is always there: the Father of Jesus, as great in love as in power.

This is the day that God has made. I will rejoice and be glad in it. I will think about God's light, joy, and power, and myself as God's beloved child. I will *run* on God's errands—still God's, though so ordinary and so repetitive. Done for God they will be *extra-*ordinary. I will make them as perfect as possible.

As I meditate, though only for five or seven un-hurried minutes in the morning, it will bless me in the moment and sink down into my subconscious to bless me a hundredfold when it rises again in an hour of special need.

Imagine having a subconscious stored with trea-sure like that, richly accumulating from a daily de-posit! Imagine being ready to turn the mind over to meditation whenever one is kept waiting: not fuming and fretting for the bus that does not come—and get-ting worse for doing it!—but dwelling on the peace that will seep into one at any time by the turning of a thought. Holiness, freedom, power, peace, light, joy, beauty, wisdom, love—all are key words for med-itation; all are attributes of the living God; and all of them, as I dwell on them in God, rest in my own soul, too.

Prayer and meditation—these are the ways to in-

timacy with Jesus, and of Jesus we can say with
Charles Wesley:

> Jesus, my all in all Thou art;
>   My rest in toil, my ease in pain,
> The medicine of my broken heart,
>   In war my peace, in loss my gain,
> My smile beneath the tyrant's frown,
> In shame my glory and my crown:
> In want my plentiful supply,
>   In weakness my almighty power,
> In bonds my perfect liberty,
>   My light in Satan's darkest hour,
> In grief my joy unspeakable,
>   My life in death, my heaven in hell.

PART II

How to Form a Prayer Cell

Honest and continual prayer expresses faith and proves its presence. Moreover, it *nourishes* the faith it expresses. When we pray with other people, God has as many avenues to our minds as we have friends who are God's friends. Insights are shared and the fire moves from heart to heart.

—*W. E. Sangster*

Part II:
How to Form a Prayer Cell

❧

Prayer and Revival

The Christian Church in England is in the shadows. No more than ten to fifteen per cent of the population are in vital touch with any branch of it. It is this neglect of God that is partly responsible for the high divorce rate and the increase of crime and juvenile delinquency.

Most devout people who have studied the problem doubt the possibility of change unless the people who still sustain the Church can reach a higher level of convinced, persistent, and corporate prayer. Something seems to be added to prayers offered in fellowship that is not available in the same measure when the same prayers are offered by the same people in separation.

If—for every important reason that requires it—we want to see the Christian religion revived among us, we must learn how to multiply the number of prayer cells or prayer groups. This portion of the book aims at telling you why—and how.

THE BIBLE COMMENDS IT

1. Jesus Commands It

"Where two or three are gathered in my name, I am there among them." (Matthew 18:20)

"Ask, and it will be given you; search, and you will find; knock, and the door will be opened for you." (Matthew 7:7)

"If two of you agree on earth about anything you ask, it will be done for you by my Father in heaven." (Matthew 18:19)

2. Paul Urges It

"I desire, then, that in every place the men should pray, lifting up holy hands." (1 Timothy 2:8)

"Pray in the Spirit at all times in every prayer and supplication." (Ephesians 6:18)

"In everything by prayer and supplication with

thanksgiving let your requests be made known to God." (Philippians 4:6)

3. The Early Church Practiced It

"All these were constantly devoting themselves to prayer." (Acts 1:14)

"When they had prayed, the place in which they were gathered together was shaken; and they were all filled with the Holy Spirit." (Acts 4:31)

"He went to the house . . . where many had gathered and were praying." (Acts 12:12)

HISTORY CONFIRMS IT

In the history of the Christian Church there have been recurrent periods of advance and retreat, of shine and shade. Some scholars have given special study to the causes of the changes and what means, in particular, God has employed to move in power upon God's people.

All are agreed that revival is an act of God. But seeing that God never acts unreasonably, we have wondered what were the reasons why God acted here, and not there; then, and not now?

Normally, God has an able and utterly consecrated individual who responds to God's touch and is filled with the Holy Spirit, *but there are records of revival without a dominating personality.*

Often the leader has a consecrated colleague who can put the spoken message into lilting music and thrilling song. John Wesley had his brother Charles, and Dwight Moody had his Ira Sankey. *But there are records of revival without a new burst of spiritual song.*

What, however, appears to be common to every deep revival of religion is a prelude of pleading, passionate, and persistent prayer. Those who had remained true to God might have been but a remnant, yet they were that kind of remnant. They *believed* and they *prayed.* To that quality of praying God responded. There is no known revival without this prelude of prayer.

REASON ENDORSES IT

It seems strange to some people that the mighty help of God should come first through our praying; they would have expected it, rather, as a result of deep thinking, hard working, or large giving.

But prayer is first. We can see why. It proves that we have already a measure of faith. Unbelievers do not really pray. Honest and continual prayer expresses faith and proves its presence. Moreover, it *nourishes* the faith it expresses; and when we pray with other people, God has as many avenues to our minds as we have friends who are God's friends too. Insights are shared and the fire moves from heart to heart.

Thinking, working, and giving all follow from this. We must be intimate with God before we can "think straight," know what to work for, or how and when to give. What awful waste of thought and work and money there is in this world *all because they are not preceded by the right quality of prayer.*

Prayer must be first. Its chief fruit is fellowship with God, and only those who know God have much to give of lasting worth to their neighbors.

Even the *problems* of prayer yield to the practice of it. I learned to pray as I learned to swim. I got into the water.

BUT WE RESIST IT

Prayer is a formality with many Christian people— their private prayers as well as their prayers in church. They maintain them more from duty than delight, and sometimes because of a superstitious suspicion that it might be "bad luck" to drop them altogether. The idea of prayer as the highest privilege and chief occupation of the day sounds secretly silly to them. But they are the silly ones! If prayer is fellowship with the almighty God of this universe, how can it be other than the chief business and privilege of every day? The people to be pitied are the people who neglect it altogether, or observe prayer only in this stunted and superstitious way.

Periodically, the leaders of the churches issue a call for more prayer. Invariably, it meets with an inadequate response. A local church here or there may do something about it; but, for the most part, it is treated with a brief respect and a long indifference.

The need is patent. The cure is plain. *But the people will not pray!*

YET WE MUST DO IT

Will you do something about this?

YOU—man or woman, young or old, rich or poor, sick or well? You do not need to be a born leader, nor a *very* deep Bible student, nor a person of position or status. This is work for any sincere and serious Christian. You must already have some conviction about prayer to have read so far in this book. Does God want you to do something about this? God's Church languishes for lack of prayer. The gates of hell prevail against us for lack of prayer. The Kingdom is impeded in its coming for lack of prayer. *You* could be of service to God, to the nation, and to the world if you would form or help to form a prayer cell. It might be the most useful thing you have done in your life.

Are you a convinced Christian and a member of God's Church? Do you share this conviction that if the number of prayer groups were multiplied, the power of God could flood into this needy world? Why not be quiet before God and inquire God's will for you? Anyone can do this thing who cares enough. *Caring* is the key word—caring for the purpose of God, caring for other people, caring that you make a maximum of your own life.

If you care enough, let us see how you might go about it.

WHO?

If you are willing to work with God in this way, commit yourself afresh to God. If you think it would help you, give yourself a *spiritual check-up*.

Now raise with God the question whether you should join some prayer group already in existence or start one. If you are led to start one—there may be no group you *could* join—inquire of God to what *one* person you should mention the matter first.

Pray further about the conversation, seek a suitable time and have an unhurried talk with that person. Tell him or her how God has led you, why you think united prayer so important, and what you hope may come of this venture.

If—at once or after reflection—the other person agrees to join with you, you have a prayer cell. Two are enough: "Where two or three are gathered in my name. . . ." Ten or twelve might be regarded as maximum. If the cell gets bigger, divide it. If there are too many members, you cannot know one another at a depth, and a prayer cell should be an intimate fellowship.

But how does the prayer cell of two become ten?

In the same way as the one became two! Let the two pray together about whom they should ask to join. Let the invitation usually be given in private talk—one with one. Let each prospective member know what the whole idea is, how God inspired it, and how God can use it.

The person who begins it need not be the "leader." Some prayer cells have no leader; each member leads in turn. But every cell has a dedicated personality at its heart—someone rich in love, fostering the life of the cell, focusing the "caring" that is at the heart of it all.

This work does not require a genius—just someone deeply in love with Jesus.

WHERE?

Prayer cells can live almost anywhere, but the place where they are formed inevitably affects their membership. Here are four kinds:

1. A Family Prayer Cell

Even in Christian homes it is sometimes hard to maintain a full service of family prayer, but even in the busiest home three or four minutes can be found after the meal of the day at which everyone meets. In the family prayer cell I know best, the members bow their heads at table every day with two things in mind: especial gratitude and pleading petition.

2. A Business Prayer Cell

Most businesses of any size include Christian people. It is an advantage if they belong to varied denominations; each can learn from the other. Half an hour at lunch time, once or twice a week, can do much for the factory, the warehouse, the office, or the shop.

3. A Neighborhood Prayer Cell

Christian housewives meet in some areas in one another's homes once a week at midmorning coffee or for a cup of afternoon tea. The tea or coffee is dispatched in a few minutes—but the forty minutes of Christian fellowship and prayer is spiritual life to them.

4. A Church Prayer Cell

It need not meet at the church. It can meet in the members' homes, but happy is that earnest minister whose church is rich with many prayer cells. That minister's dreams will come true.

WHEN?

The place of the prayer cell almost decides the time of its meeting. The family prayer cell, as we have said, can use a few minutes daily at the meal at which all the members of the family are present. If there are children in the family, they can be drawn into this quite naturally—especially if they are allowed to make suggestions on the themes for praying.

Prayer cells in a business house or factory meet with naturalness during the lunch hour or when work ends. These cells must be careful to avoid the appearance of being exclusive cliques with a "holier-than-thou" manner. All the members of the cell should commend their religion, first, by being good at their jobs, eager, kind, and helpful.

Neighborhood prayer cells meet weekly entirely at the convenience of the members, and those cells composed mainly of homemakers can easily study the claims upon them of spouses and children. Mid-morning and mid-afternoon are the most popular times in these groups.

A church prayer cell is clearly free to fix its own time. Respect will be paid, of course, to other established church meetings—even though nothing shakes our conviction that prayer is the greatest need of all. In some churches the meeting is held every *eighth* day so that no one is regularly shut out.

HOW?

There are four ways of corporate prayer, and God has blessed them all. Any talk about one being better than the others is silly.

1. Silent Prayer

Remember that this is silent prayer in *fellowship*. You are in the company of others who are mentally praying, too. But the commerce with heaven is all in the secrecy of the soul.

2. Read Prayer

The greatest part of the world's corporate praying is in liturgical form and the prayers are read. Many of the prayers are very beautiful and seem to hold the distilled devotion of the centuries. Yet you need not borrow your prayers if you want to read them. You can write and read your own.

3. Bidding Prayer

In bidding prayer, the leader offers the theme to the members of the cell. She or he suggests, "Let us pray for . . ." and many add a vivid sentence or two (not more) to enliven the sense of urgency and quicken the desire to pray for the particular need or person. The actual prayers are offered in silence, though the leader may gather them together in a sentence of spoken prayer at the end.

4. Free Prayer

Here is prayer, vocal, spontaneous, leaping from the heart and lips, unguided, except by the Holy Spirit, and poured out as the needs of others and of the world rise in the mind of the one at prayer. Almost all prayer cells come to include free prayer.

These *four ways* are all owned of God. Happy are the members of the prayer cell who know how to use them *all* and who remember one another in prayer every day. Happy are they, also, if they conclude their weekly meeting with the word *action*, and ask God how they can help to answer their own prayers.

PREPARING TO PRAY

The lack of seriousness about corporate prayer displays itself not only in its neglect, but also—oddly enough—in its practice.

One reason why the old prayer meeting died was a certain casualness and a tiresome repetition of the same prayers by the same people. Employing mainly free prayer, people seemed to speak to God with less forethought than they would use in conversation with another human being, and often darted in a disordered way from one subject to another as it chanced to occur to their mind.

Prayer demands premeditation. In a well-conducted prayer cell, people talk first about the objectives of their praying, and may even keep minutes of their agreed decisions. Prayer aims need classifying. We know God wants to revive sound religion among us, but some things need checking. Is this a thing we *ought* to pray for? Are we sure God wants to give us these things, and can we pray affirmatively: "We know, Father, that you are pouring your comfort on our bereaved friend . . ."? Or are there matters in which we are not yet sure of the divine will: "Father, if it be your will, grant that our friend may secure that coveted appointment . . ."?

On many issues, only quiet fellowship and conversation with one another and with God clears the mind, saves us from selfishness in our praying, widens our concerns, fixes the priorities, and gives God the chance to shape God's wishes in our hearts. God's power moves to God's ends. It is only when we are praying in the Spirit that we can have whatever we ask.

PLEADING THE CASE

There is another reason, also, why we should not assemble in a prayer cell and start talking to God at once. Even if the prayer aims are clear from previous agreement, and are refreshed in the memory by a word of reminder, the realization of God's presence, which is so necessary to effective praying, also requires a period of quiet.

People unpracticed in prayer and troubled by their wandering thoughts sometimes ask for help here. "What do you do," they almost inquire, "with your mind in silent prayer?"

First, think of God—God's greatness, goodness,

love, mercy, eagerness, and ability to meet every need. Think of God. However much the mind wanders, the moment you are aware that it is astray, firmly bring it back once more. Think of God. Never begrudge the moments it takes to realize God's presence. When you are at the "central point of bliss," the requests can be briefly and confidently made.

Then think about the agreed themes for prayer, taking each in turn. If you are asking for someone's healing, do not see them sick or feel their pain. See them *well*. Imagine God's perfect will for them in your mind. In your thinking and in your longing, loving heart, unite God in God's power to bless with the object of your prayer in his or her need. Join them. At times you almost feel the blessing flowing through.

Praying for nations and large social causes is very important but not easy. Most experts in prayer advise us to select "key people" involved in the situations, learn all we can of their need, and focus our praying on them.

WATCHING IT WORK

People who persist in prayer do not doubt its worth. The practice, as we have said, answers most of the problems. If a few remain—well, having heard God speak, we can bear divine silence. God will tell us some day.

The personal gains alone are enormous. By prayer we learn to know God. Everything else depends upon that. If you are sure of God, what matters? By prayer we learn to love others—even those who are hard to like—and our thinking is sounder, clearer, larger. By prayer we can carry our crosses with courage and look quietly in the face of death.

But the gains are wider than our personal lives. By prayer homes have been transformed, relationships in business sweetened, civic and social affairs made wholesome, and the life of churches changed from impotence into enormous spiritual power. Remember to give the revival of deep religion among us a priority in all your praying.

What prayer could do in the life of the nation and the world has never really been tried. Millions of people neglect it because they think it is just pious talk and we ought to be "up and doing something." To what chaos has their "up and doing" led! Only when people listen to God can they learn what they should be "up and doing". If they would listen in prayer and obey God's bidding, then, in the words of the old hymn, "earth might be fair, and all men glad and wise."

TEACH ME TO PRAY

Not for myself alone
    May my prayer be;
Lift Thou Thy world, O Christ,
    Closer to Thee!
Cleanse it from guilt and wrong;
Teach it salvation's song,
Till earth, as heaven, fulfill
God's holy will.

           —Lucy Larcom

GO TO IT

What are you going to do about it?

The Bible commends it, history confirms it, reason endorses it, the nation and the Church need it. Will *you* join or start a prayer cell?

Do not say you do not *feel* like it!

This does not depend on feeling. It is the fruit of a resolute act of will. The feeling will come later. There is hardly anybody who has read and understood this book who could not do something about it. I have known the bedridden to form a prayer cell.

Will *you*? At home? at school or college? at business? in the neighborhood? at church?

Whom will you speak to first?

The responsibility is now squarely on you.

PART III

How to Live In Christ

I have been crucified with Christ; and it is no longer I who live, but it is Christ who lives in me. And the life I now live in the flesh I live by faith in the Son of God, who loved me and gave himself for me.

—*Galatians 2:19, 20*

Part III: How to Live in Christ

❧

Introduction

hat does the phrase "Live in Christ" mean?

It sounds quite fuzzy and vague.

Yet in his thirteen letters—most of them brief—St. Paul speaks of being "in Christ" or having Christ "in us" many times. It must have meant an enormous lot to him.

Does it mean, then, something quite real and sensible; something practical and full of common sense; something wonderful and life-transforming; something central to the Christian faith and possible to everyone?

It means all those things. It is the open secret of the Christian life and the single substantial hope of personal and world change.

Only as Christ really lives in more and more people can men and women be altered and the world saved from disaster. In itself and in its consequences, it is the most important subject to which mortals could turn their minds.

WHY SHOULD ONE LIVE IN CHRIST?

We mortals do most of our living inside ourselves.

Our life is made up mainly of thinking, feeling, and willing. Though the world and other people press upon us, thinking, feeling, and willing remain our essential life. Even the outward pressures upon us can only reach us in this threefold way.

Unhappily, normal human nature is self-centered. Unless people are spiritually remade, everything that comes up is seen from a selfish angle. "I . . . I . . . I . . . Me . . . Me . . . Me!" Self is central and self is demanding.

People are unhappy and the world is a near hell because people are so self-centered. It makes them greedy, proud, and pushy. For generations the best people have been trying to put themselves right— and failing. The testimony of those who have tried hardest and gone furthest is that we cannot save ourselves.

The great perplexity of humanity has resolved itself, therefore, into this: "Is there a power or a Person in the universe who can come into human nature and radically change it—who can shift the center from self to something or Someone higher; who can think and feel and will within us, and make us what we can never make ourselves; who can break our self-obsession and somehow set us free?"

Christianity claims that is what is meant by having Christ living in us and by our living in Christ.

IS IT POSSIBLE TO LIVE IN CHRIST?

Christ said to his disciples: "Abide in me as I abide in you. Just as the branch cannot bear fruit by itself unless it abides in the vine, neither can you, unless you abide in me." Clearly, definitely, and repeatedly Jesus told them that it was possible for him to live within them, and for them to live in him.

But even a word uttered with such enormous authority would still leave us wistfully uncertain if no man or woman had ever experienced this indwelling life.

But they did! They wrote of it. Paul's letters, as we have remarked already, are full of it. With so many other important things to say, he says one thing over and over again. "In Christ," "Christ in you," he says many times! It was his "magnificent obsession." It is not help from without, but power from within. It is the central secret of all truly spiritual religion—the life of God in the human soul.

Millions have known it throughout the centuries. *The Imitation of Christ* and *The Practice of the Presence of God* speak of it in different ways.

You can have it, too!

HOW DOES IT HAPPEN?

To the natural mind, the idea of anybody else living *in* us seems plain silly or a bit of religious mumbo-jumbo. "How can anybody else live in me?" the person on the street asks, without even waiting for an answer. To suggest the possibility proves (it seems) that you are crazy.

Perhaps the only way to convince someone of the possibility is to display this quality of life yourself. The life of Christ is so potent, so radiant, so engaging that people cannot resist it. When they really see the appearance of his life in us, it fascinates and holds them.

How, then, does this life come in? What must people do who, being forgiven by God and truly trusting Christ, want that divine life in their own stunted souls?

They must believe in its *possibility*. The promise of

Christ, the testimony of the apostles, the experience of the Church must wipe unbelief from the mind.

They must want it *ardently*. God is drawn into our souls by "the lure of strong desire." Desire is inflamed by constant study of the life of Christ in the New Testament. Desire is inflamed also by the study of the saints. Desire is inflamed by prayer. Just to think on him and murmur his name, "Jesus! Jesus!" increases the longing.

They must open their *minds* to Christ's incoming. Because this is not as simple as it sounds, it is here that they need special help.

GIVING OUR MIND TO CHRIST

All the conscious part of receiving the life of God in the human soul takes place in our mind. We cannot receive the life of God as a medicine or an injection. All that *we* can do is within our mind.

We *want* to have Christ. Our feelings are set that way. As we give him our *mind*, our feelings increase and our will is more set. But how can we give him our mind?

Is it as hard as that? All our school days our teachers urged us "to give our minds" to things. There is nothing mysterious here. It is all summarized in the word *attention*. We give our mind to Christ when we pay attention to him, think of him, talk to him, work with him, rest with him, walk with him—and the more we give him our minds, the more he gives us his.

It would shock many Christians if an angel were to tell them how few the moments are in any day when they really give their mind to Christ. Not even the moments given to prayer are fully given to him. Take from those skimpy minutes the time consumed by wandering of mind and selfish pleading for this and that. How little is left for that absorbed and desiring contemplation of God in which the real transfer of divine life takes place.

Is it any wonder that, even among those of us who profess and call ourselves Christians, there are so few who convincingly reveal our Lord?

NO SHORT CUTS—NOT EVEN HOLY ONES

So it is as simple and as hard as that! We just pay attention to Christ, and he does the rest. So eager is he to give himself to us that if we only give our minds to him—in he comes. Why do we pay so little attention to him? Do we not believe that it *could* be? Do we not want it enough?

There are people who readily concede that one

must give hours a week to learn shorthand or some foreign language, but think that the life of God can be picked up in a few breathless moments a day.

It cannot! It is free but it involves discipline—the discipline of truly paying attention to Christ. If we want this, we must learn how to give him our minds. We must be resolute, methodical, and eager. We must see it as the chief business of every day. We must borrow and adapt the methods of the saints and welcome or invent new techniques—and all to one end: so to give Christ our mind that he may give us his.

One of the reasons why the gospel has not spread as it should is because people who claim to have it do not "sell" it by the way they live.

Many professing Christians completely fail to impress worldly people with their possession of some priceless secret. They seem as worried and frustrated as the people who never give a thought to God at all.

Two errors are common among Christians in relation to this indwelling life. Some believe that if they can repeat the right theological words they are clearly "in Christ," and some believe that if they closely observe the services of the Church—especially the sacrament of Holy Communion—they, also, are clearly "in Christ" and he is in them.

It is hard to exaggerate the importance of sound

theological statements or the value of the sacrament Christ instituted himself. It is only necessary to say with sadness that even sound formulas can become "just words" and the most solemn symbols handled with such formality that it is little more than going through the motions. Neither right formulas nor regular sacraments guarantee of themselves the indwelling life. Used correctly, they can both be aids to it. But it is possible to repeat the creeds and attend the sacrament and not receive the mind of Christ.

He gives us his mind as we really give him ours. How can we help one another so to give our minds to Christ that he can give his life to us?

GETTING DOWN TO THE DAY-TO-DAY

We are aiming, then, to give our mind to Christ.

We are appalled to realize how few of the 960 waking minutes of every day are *really* given to him.

We have our work to do, and we realize that the degree of our concentration must vary with the hours of the day.

But we know that even when our minds are necessarily concentrated on the most material things, our work can all be offered to Christ and the background of our thinking still be about him.

We know, also, that there must be no strain about this. A strained life cannot reflect the repose of Jesus.

But why should we be strained? It is not as though we were really doing it. We look to Christ. We think about him. We walk and talk and sing with him. But *he* it is who does things. He chose the apostles "to be with him," and they grew like him. So may we!

To our morning quiet time (Bible-study and prayer) we are adding this exciting venture. We are going to see how much of every day we can think about Christ. There will be solemn moments, of course, but many more joyful ones because he is such an enjoyable Companion. People may be a bit surprised at us on occasion because the discerning ones will guess that there is something different about us. As Christ comes into us, other people will be drawn to us because he is literally the most attractive Being in the universe.

We will seek his help to make this companionship so much second nature that the day will come when we shall really understand what Paul meant when he said, "It is no longer I who live, but it is Christ who lives in me."

ON WAKING

Turn your mind at once to Christ. If you wake slowly, let each step to wakefulness be a step toward him. Address to him your first words of the day. Say in your heart: "I am here, Lord, and eager for another day."

Cultivate the custom of linking your Lord and yourself with "We." "What are we going to do together today, Lord?" If it seems too familiar at first, remember that he encourages such intimacy. It is beyond understanding why he should want to live in our soiled hearts—but *he does*, and this united life is made easier with the plural pronoun. Say "We."

Glance ahead at the day. "We are going to do everything together today, Lord." See yourself going through the day with him. Meet every known duty in thought with him before you meet it (still with him) in reality. "We must make the most of that opportunity, Lord." "We must be particularly watchful there, Lord. . . ."

Then rise with zest and begin your day. These are the first steps of the indwelling life. Murmur the prayer:

> Come nearer, Lord, than near me
> My succor to begin:
> Usurp the heart that craves Thee!
> O come and dwell within.

AT THE TABLE

The Quakers believe that all meals should be sacramental. We can make them so if we take them with our Lord.

It is not hard to do this. We have but to call him to our minds—and he shares the meal.

Any meal with him is beautifully different. Jesus was the kind of person people loved to have at a party.

Conversation with him has insight, depth, range, and sparkle, too. He is not always (or usually) talking "religion," and *we* must not. Living the indwelling life does not turn all our talk into sermons!

But wounding criticism of others will go from the conversation, and the cold boredom with one another that many families endure will go as well. One person at the table consciously thinking of Christ's presence would make a difference in a week and might make a transformation in a month.

Have grace at meals if you can—and sometimes turn it into a little prayer. A birthday, the children facing examination, news from a friend in a morning letter—many things provide the substance of a sentence prayer. It is a family acknowledgment of Christ's presence and will help others in the home who also want to live "in him."

Now let the chatter loose! Food with the Lord can be fun.

GOING TO WORK

It is in the intervals of our day that weakening and self-obsessing thoughts can take possession of us. It is when we have no need to be concentrated and thought can dart where it will that it often darts to fear, fret, and self-absorption.

Going to work is such a time. There is no need to concentrate on the journey. You know it all so well. Go to work in Jesus. Talk with him as you go.

Pray for the people you pass in the street and sit by in the bus or on the train. How sad so many people seem when their faces are in repose! What secret cares are gnawing at them? Turn the widest stream of God's love on them that can channel its way through your narrow but broadening heart. It will unconsciously bless them as they travel with you because they are traveling with Christ!

Enter your place of business with your Lord. See the people you work with through the eyes of the Savior. You have brought Christ with you to work; and your colleagues, though all unaware, are going to work with the Master. How long before they find out? How long, at least, till they know there is something strangely different about you? How long before they ask themselves: "What's she or he got that I haven't got?"

Some people are not easy to work with. Am I easy to work with? If the fault is all in them, how would Jesus look at them? How much allowance would he make for the secret hurts and disappointments that have made them what they are? One thing is certain: Christ would not allow their abruptness or bad manners to make him bad-mannered, too. He would still look on them in his Father's love.

IN THE HOME

Homemakers do not have to *go* to work. They get up in the morning and the work is all around them!

But no work surpasses theirs in importance. Christian homes are our great need.

How would Christ run a home? What would he have more than good meals, cleanliness, and modest comfort? How would he shop or run errands?

Homemakers whose longing desire it is to have Christ living within them have advantages and disadvantages. So much of their work is mechanical. The preparation of meals, the making of beds, cleaning the room, washing up—the same things over and over again.

When one is busy with habitual work that only takes a tenth of the mind, the rest of the mind, as we have seen, wanders off on its own: to fears of sickness, failure, loss of love; or to day-dreams of sudden wealth, ample leisure, greater charm. . . .

The battle for those who would live in Christ is set here. Hours of all our lives—though especially of those whose work is tedious—are subject to this fantastical thinking. Do not let thought wander to fear and fret and self and sin. Gently draw it to Christ. School yourself to the point where every thought released from necessary concentration darts back at once to the Beloved.

Talk to Jesus as you work. Sing to him. The deep hymns—and the not-so-deep—either will do so long as they center in him.

I serve a risen Savior, he's in the world today. . . .
My Jesus, I love thee, I know thou art mine. . . .
Take the name of Jesus with you. . . .

AT WORK ITSELF

The first duty of the Christian at work is to be a good worker; not to persuade others to go to church, or "to give up drinking," or to be converted—but to be a good worker. And this applies whether you are in the office or on the factory floor.

While there are parts of all people's work that are half-habitual and can be done with the mind on something else (or some-One else), the more highly skilled the work the more concentration it requires. The duty of Christians at such work is to put their *whole* mind to it. The operation is in process . . . the experiment is on the way . . . the speech is being made. Nothing less than the whole mind is engaged.

Living with Christ does not weigh against that concentration. It adds to it. Work approached after prayer (and done with Christ) is more concentrated, more complete, and more effective than any work done on your own. The increased sense of effectiveness is enormous and can only be imagined by those who have not experienced it.

This must be said, too. To that complete sense of concentration is added an exhilarating sense of co-operation. One *knows* one is not alone. "My hand is held by Another. Another is thinking in me. Somebody else is looking through my eyes. . . ." The sense of aid increases with the gravity of the work. As soon as the need for absorbed concentration is over, one turns one's whole mind again to intimate talk with the beloved Colleague and whispers: "We did that well, Lord, and we did it together." Though we have contributed but a thousandth part of the whole, he smiles and says, "*We did!*"

IN SCHOOL

Living with Christ is not for adults only. Growing children can be taught the simple technique. When the years of serious schooling come and young people are giving their minds to many subjects, it is not really hard to teach them how to give their minds to Christ.

Children are more spiritually sensitive than we realize. Nothing we could do for our children would be more precious than to teach them simply, naturally, and out of experience what it is to live in Christ.

Learning with Jesus makes favorite lessons fun and hard lessons possible. It can help young people to look upon study not as "a bore" but as a privilege. It can bring them to a classroom whispering to their Lord: "Let us make the most of our time, Lord. Let us clear and concentrate and stay our mind on the work."

Games are not outside our Lord's interest. Gone are the days when people thought that God was only interested in them when they were reading the Bible or saying their prayers. It is fine to teach young people to go on the field or tennis court with their Lord;

to win if possible but—win or lose—to play eagerly, cleanly, and with unfailing good humor.

An educational missionary in India who taught this way of life to his boys knew that he was succeeding on the day when one of his lads scored his first goal in soccer. As he saw the ball shoot from his bare foot to the corner of the net, the boy revealed his inner and intimate companionship as he cried with delight: "Look! Lord Jesus, look!"

IN THE EVENING HOURS

The evening hours for most people are hours of leisure. We may spend them in the family circle, or pursuing a hobby, or in the service of God and God's Church, or widening our education, or enjoying some entertainment. More than most hours in the day, these, we feel, are our own.

No time is really our own. All is Christ's. It is not *our* time, some of which we give to him. It is *his* time, and he is glad to give leisure to us.

Living with Christ means that we cannot go anywhere we cannot go with him—but that does not limit us to church. All wholesome life is his.

Some people find it hard to be their best at home. They treat those they claim to love with less courtesy than they treat strangers.

Christ within us alters all that. Caring for others becomes our "second nature"—because it is *his* nature. Family life is enormously enriched when Christ is always there.

As the day draws to its close, and we remember that we have not done all we had hoped, we shall remember also that our chief business every day is not to fill the hours as full as possible, but to let Christ fill us with himself.

ON GOING TO BED

As the day comes to its close and you are composing your mind for sleep, run back over the day with your Lord. Yes! *With* him. Remember, the aim is everything together! And you are still together as you pass the day in review.

Roughly assess how much he has been in your mind during the day. There will be much to be happy about, and even more with passing time. As you build this technique into the very structure of your days, it will become more and more habitual—and all the better for that. The bits you do on your own will be fewer. Far as you may be from all you desire, you will draw daily nearer the identified life.

"We took *that* opportunity, Lord!" "We helped *them!*" "We got *that* sorted out!" "We know the next steps. . . ." Again and again, the heart will swell with thanksgiving as the certainty of Christ's companionship fills the mind again.

But there will be other moments in the review, too; embarrassing, humbling, even scorching moments. We shall remember things he had no part in. Hurtful things we said; unchristian deeds and thoughts. . . . Sometimes we will be silenced with shame or find ourselves faintly whispering, "I did that alone."

Claim Christ's forgiveness. We can all slip *but we must not wallow*. When you can do so, lift yourself up. And do so as soon as you can. Then go on living the indwelling life—humbler, less assertive, and more Christ-centered than ever.

But not all life is lived in a day.

There come special periods when we specially need the nearness of our Lord.

IN LOVE

When we fall in love is such a time; indeed, *before* we fall, that we may "fall" the right way!

What wide unhappiness is common in the world because people link their lives with the wrong partner. It is part of the inescapable difficulty of life that we must make life's greatest decisions at the time of life's great inexperience. Choosing life's partner is one of those decisions.

If Christ is reigning within, we cannot be deeply attracted to the wrong people or fail to be chaste before we are wed and faithful afterward.

IN SPECIAL PROBLEMS

When Christ lives within us, we have seen that he thinks and feels and wills in his consenting servant.

The way he thinks with us is a most exciting experience for people who brood on the problems of life.

One raises a subject with Christ and he discusses it within the mind. He asks questions, helps one to inferences, draws out the answers—sometimes from one's own mind and sometimes by a gleam of revelation. Often in these absorbed conversations in the soul it is not easy to remember who asked the question and who answered it. That does not matter. Thinking alone and thinking with Christ are poles apart.

IN SORROW

Sooner or later, sorrow comes to us all.

Sometimes it is devastating. A dear one is taken from us or certified insane. The looked-for baby arrives but has severe birth defects. A love we thought was constant proves brittle. How is it then with the Christ within? Can Christ live in a heart tempted to believe that he has forgotten to be gracious?

The testimony of those who have walked this way is that Christ is never so precious as now, that the most tender human sympathy is insensitive beside his, that he can enter into our torn heart and "soothe and hush and calm it. . . ."

Other humans soon tire of our sorrow and grow weary of our longing to talk about our loved one. He does not! He loves the loved one deeply, too.

IN SUCCESS

It is commonly accepted by moralists that prosperity is more dangerous than adversity and that more people have failed through success than through anything else.

It is not hard to understand. If people believe themselves to be the architects of their own success, they get inflated. If Christ is not ruling within, it is easy to see how the assertive self swells with the business, or the social distinction, or whatever it is that constitutes the ground of pride. The ego, eager to boast about anything, is doubly eager to blast on the trumpet when there is something wonderful like this . . . !

Only Christ within can save us from this. He alone, in his lovely personal conversations, can convince us that we have nothing we do not owe to his grace.

IN SICKNESS

If the most effective thing mortals can do in the service of the world is so to give themselves to Christ that he may live again in them, then the sick can serve him no less than the healthy.

The poor twisted arthritic is not cut out; the lame, deaf, blind, and paralyzed may enlist as well.

Some sicknesses are cured by Christ's presence and all are helped. But with many there is a burden still to be borne.

How bravely they bear it who bear it with him. How wonderfully they serve him who take the cup, as he did, from his Father's hand. "God *permits* this. . . ." "God can use it." I have known invalids who were denied the healing they asked for become mighty in full-time intercession and deeply wise with counsel they had received from their Lord.

AS THE SHADOWS LENGTHEN

Life narrows in some ways as we grow older.

Things have to be given up. They are "beyond us." We know the hurt of waning powers.

There are gains in this. We have more time for those secret conversations with our indwelling Lord; more time, as he guides us, for others; a truer sense of values.

How dull and undesirable in the evening light some things appear that seemed so important to us when the sun was climbing the sky!

But to talk unhurriedly with Jesus in whose safe-keeping many of our dear ones already are—Oh, what bliss! And there is service still to be done! Some have done their best work in the evening hours.

AT THE THOUGHT OF DEATH

I think that five people out of seven over fifty years of age are thinking of death.

Not *talking* of it. Oh, no! They would regard that

as morbid. But *thinking* of it. "A number of friends have gone. . . . It will be my turn one of these days. . . . What will it be? A stroke, cancer, or senility?" Some are stoical, some pretend to be indifferent, and some, like O'Henry, are "afraid to go home in the dark."

But to those in whom Christ dwells there is no fearful apprehension. The more intimate they have become with him, the less foreboding do they feel about their departure. "You have trusted me in life," he says. "Trust me in death."

So they trust him. They know no need he does not meet. To live in Christ is to live forever. To die is gain.

TO KEEP CHRIST IN MIND-

Pray. . . . Go for a walk with Jesus. . . . Use affirmations to yourself: "I am his and he is mine"; "My Jesus I love thee, I know thou art mine"; "Then sings my soul, my Savior God to thee; how great thou art. . . ." Use imagination. See yourself remade in Christ. . . . Keep a devotional corner in your room. . . . Have a picture of your Lord in view. . . . As you turn in your work from one major task to another, offer a silent prayer for help to do it well. . . . Learn to listen to him. . . . Cultivate instant obedience to any suggestion he makes. . . . Keep a set of words—love, joy, peace, patience—in the back of your mind for meditation when the mind starts to wander off to fret and to self. . . . Do not *push* him into conversations with others but take the natural openings. . . . Think about those you know who most resemble Christ. . . . But, above all, *think about Christ.*

Further Reading

For Part I

Thomas à Kempis, *The Imitation of Christ*
William Law, *A Serious Call to a Devout and Holy Life*
Douglas Steere, *Dimensions of Prayer*
Maxie Dunnam, *The Workbook of Living Prayer* and
    The Workbook of Intercessory Prayer
Timothy Jones, *The Art of Prayer: A Simple Guide*

For Part II

Norvene Vest, *Gathered in the Word: Praying the Scripture in Small Groups*
Rueben Job and Norman Shawchuck, *A Guide to Prayer for Ministers and Other Servants* and *A Guide to Prayer for All God's People*

For Part III

Brother Lawrence, *The Practice of the Presence of God*
Thomas Kelly, *A Testament of Devotion*
Maxie Dunnam, *The Workbook on Becoming Alive in Christ*